RISK THE PIER

RISK

THE

PIER

Shelley
Roche-Jacques

 EYEWEAR PUBLISHING

First published in 2017
by Eyewear Publishing Ltd
Suite 333, 19-21 Crawford Street
Marylebone, London w1h 1pj
United Kingdom

Cover design and typeset by Edwin Smet
Author photograph by Sean Jacques

Printed in England by TJ International Ltd, Padstow, Cornwall

ISBN 978-1-911335-98-6

Eyewear wishes to thank Jonathan Wonham for his
generous patronage of our press.

WWW.EYEWEARPUBLISHING.COM

For Mum, Dad and Simon,
and in memory of Linda Moody

Shelley Roche-Jacques'
poetry has appeared in magazines such as
Magma, The Rialto, The Interpreter's House and
The Boston Review. Her pamphlet *Ripening Dark*
was published in 2015 as part of the Eyewear
20/20 series. She has performed her work widely,
collaborating with actors, musicians and other
poets. She teaches Creative Writing at Sheffield
Hallam University, and is particularly
interested in the dramatic monologue
as a way of examining social
and political issues.

TABLE OF CONTENTS

1.
MEN, WOMEN
AND MICE

IMPRESSION OF MY GREAT AUNT HAZEL

Once upon a time
there lived a tailoress,
parishioner, dancer
at teatime get-togethers.
She was the object of proposals,
subjected to gifts,
the speaker of refusals,
kindly put. But plumped
for the floral-clad
bosom of spinsterhood.

So no more were there bluebirds,
eager-beaked and delicate of wing,
lifting back her bedspread by its fine lace trimming.
No more snugly fitting golden slipper offers,
there-for-the-granting wishes, prophecies.
Tiny suitcases were packed:
acutely tuned narrating mice
no longer cared for singing out her life.

Just sister Ida
in the corner
with blue and twisted poison tongue.
A tailoress likewise,
but eyes like pins stabbed in.

Dog-chocolate hearted,
brother Harold did as a Harold can,
veins drawn slovenly slow
through a life lived from the frying pan.

This state not due to some stretched spell
of potion-prompted sleep;
slackened apples lay intact
in a bowl on the TV.

Her princes had all come,
been snubbed, and gone.

Impertinently she lived on,
with Ida's pin-cushion face,
Harold's queasy chuckling
and music box misplaying
Some Enchanted Evening.

SHRINK

In here I'm fine. It's watercolour prints
and plants, and wisely-chosen magazines.
I've thought all week about the goals we set.
How I must stop and think and draw deep breaths.
You said we need to figure out what triggers
the attacks. Did you call them attacks?
What's triggering the *rage*. The *incidents*.

I've really thought on that. The one at work
the other day. For God's sake! They're good guys!
Collecting for charity – dressed for a laugh
in floral blouses, lipstick, sock-stuffed bras
and heels – I guess I knew one shove would do.
I didn't mean for him to break his leg.
But he was asking for it dressed like that.

I still can't quite believe they called the police.
Second time in a week. Who knew that taking
adverts down on trains was an offence?
I had to climb onto the seats to reach,
but then the plastic casing slid clean off.
I wrenched the poster down and stared at it.
Are you beach body ready? I was not.

There's no getting away from it.
Even at night
it's all bunched up tight
in a sack of dark
above my head.
Or it stretches away
like the pier, or hospital corridor,

through the stale bedroom air
and there's me at the end of it
there – tiny –
shaking my fist silently.

But let me try to keep my focus here.
The worst of it is when I hurt my son.
A children's party is a hellish thing.
And this one had a clown who made balloons:
a flower or tiara for the girls,
swords for the boys. I didn't say a word.
I simply smiled and helped set out the food.

I nearly made it past the party games.
Musical statues. Robin Thicke. *Blurred Lines*.
There comes a time – a limit, I should say:
it's five year olds gyrating to this song.
The music stopped – I yanked my frozen son
and scrambled through the streamers to the door.
Through *You're a good girl. I know you want it.*

Unfriending soon began – and Facebook throbbed
into the night – *She calls herself a mum.*
She's fucking nuts. It's just a fucking song.
And worse, the snidey stuff, the faux concern.
It must be awful to be in that state
where something like a song can trigger that.
She has some issues. Let's give her a break.

A break! Yes please!
I'm sad face, sad face. Angry face.
The trolls of Twitter
sent me almost off the edge.
Why d'ya hate men so much @suffragette?

Look at her! Jealous!
The bitch needs shutting up.
I know where you live.
I clutched the blind,
and stared into the dark
each night for months.

I lost the fight online. Or lost the will.
I said I'd try to focus on real life.
Now that's become as messy and as grim.
I keep returning to the Town Hall steps.
I must have played that scene a thousand times.
I knew the strip club bosses would be there
in James Bond suits and aviator shades.

The dancers, I had never seen before.
I left the meeting, having said my bit
and found them waiting cross-armed on the steps.
One blocked my way, with eyes I won't forget:
so green and angry. What right did we have?
Did we want them to lose their fucking jobs?
It was alright for us – the la-di-da's.

I'm not alright. I think that's why I snapped.
I really wish that I could take it back.
I don't remember everything I said.
I'm pretty sure I mentioned self-respect
and then the men came out and shook their heads.
If I had stopped and thought and drawn deep breaths
would that have worked? What else do you suggest?

BUSY COMPANIES OF MEN

Prequel to an imagined re-boot of 'The Garden'.

'Fair Quiet, have I found thee here,
And Innocence, thy sister dear!
Mistaken long, I sought you then
In busy companies of men'
– *The Garden,* Andrew Marvell

This morning yet again you aren't
a party to the lift's ascent.
Assailed by bag and coughing wretch
I scarcely make it to my desk
but sweep the violation off
to see if you will show yourself
in trawling email sent adrift
across the night-time's slack abyss.

Beside the photocopier's plash
and idling murmur, hum and dash,
I linger, hoping to discern
the rhythm of the taciturn
and magic-eye the corporate web
of big-time bosses in vignette.
But fail to make that schema drop
the secret of each sanguine sop.

The stationery's dim-lit cove
would be a sanctum of repose
if it were not graffitied with
the evidence of baser love:
initials etched on stapleguns
and whetted pencils. With moist hands

I take the marker's dizzy notes,
peer through the windowed envelopes...

The afternoon pads lamely in
bamboozled to the fold again
but as the phone bleats off the hook
I fear you've been misdocketted
and find my heart grows weak, abhors
the long and obfuscating clause.
I rush at, snap shut and throw down
each case you have absconded from.

Relieved at five the hat-stand waves
to the precision of the safe;
its thirty-west and forty-east
the dial's dance of slick release.
I glimpse its cavern's emptiness
where spoils like precious fruit are pressed.
While in the nooks of bottom drawers
the mice begin to yawn and paw.

A cleaner starts to vacuum up.
I'll leave the dregs to fudge this mug,
the office phantom in the glass,
the city too, on bending close,
with golden arches, neon strips
and tilting, half-spent epithets.
A hive of lights that writhe and smear.
Perhaps I'm wrong to seek you here.

TO AMY LOWELL

'I only hope that possibly some day
Some other woman with an itch for writing
May turn to me as I have turned to you
And chat with me for a few brief minutes'
– *The Sisters*, Amy Lowell

I dreamt we picnicked together.
Not amid the expert horticulture of your father,
but here, in my back garden.

We spread a cloth to my tangled grass
and sprawled to flatten it and laughed
each other breathless.

Home-labelled honey,
thick bread, white currants,
a smooth brown cake with grated almonds.

All of this weird fruit
you brought. We ate, with poise,
and then you spoke:

the sapphire of our summer sky,
the tail feather of the magpie,
were not, could never be, as fine
as my shaded-pool-to-bathe-in eyes…

I smiled,
looked away,
watched an ant carry a crumb across a blue and yellow plate.

And later, in my unmown lawn,
biting finely pitted strawberries,
we marvelled at the daisies,
open-mouthed and wondering;
so unnaturally hairy-stemmed.

THE LABORATORY

'The newspapers selectively used a 'laboratory' that gave positive results where other pathology labs found none, creating an 'expert'…who worked from a garden shed.'
– Ben Goldacre, Bad Science column on MRSA, *The Guardian*

They came to me, I never looked for them
or for their money, though I needed it,
God knows. A private enterprise like this
is just a money pit – you pour it in
and watch it falling through the black – but still
I didn't always give them what they asked.
You never seemed to think to mention that –
the forty-five percent of negatives.
You talk of cherry picking with the facts
but never let me get mine all unpacked.

Remember when we first spoke on the phone
and everything was civil and you asked
me casually why all the journalists
preferred my lab, why they came back and back
and drove for miles with undercover swabs
and told their friends. I answered honestly.
I really couldn't say. I did my best.
I never told them to put *Mop of Death*
or claimed I'm *internationally renowned*.
They made that up. I was too keen, perhaps.

It's something I've been told by the bereaved,
by all the families whose pain I've eased.
They said I helped by trumpeting their cause,
by fighting to expose – I never fought...

just shone a light down filthy corridors.
But if I stopped one patient getting ill
I never did it just to sell my kits.
I could have done – I could have pushed them when
I had the eyes of all the papers – well,
it's done, they're gone, and now the loans draw in.

My interest wasn't vested like you said.
I laid it bare. Just like I answered on
the day the two inspectors came. I showed
them how I would prepare the media.
They nodded, wiped their glasses, clicked their pens.
I never said they gagged me or made threats.
They were obliged and careful on my lawn.
They shook my hand and left with promises
of contact slides. There were no *goons*. It's just
the papers thought that I'd been victimised.

And then I was. You called me names, referred
to this place as a garden shed and made
bad jokes about my non-accredited...
credentials, said I mispronounced some words
and couldn't even tell my rods from balls.
But does a garden shed have all of this?
A telephone? And I am qualified,
it's just they held me up as expert and
you know they can't be stopped once they set off
and that they love a shaggy underdog.

And now I know that's what I always was.
You beat me. After twenty years of work
you came and pulled me from my perch
just like the cat with cream...

It's cold for May.
The blossom's brown and heaped in corners and
the traffic will be jammed for hours yet
around the Northern Circular. I'll wait.
Some space to think. My apparatus creaks.
The windows of this place are dim with grime.
Are you still there? No, you've been gone some time.

LOCAL HERO FACES TIME

You say the thing that did it in the end
was a scooter thrown from the bandstand
again and again.

You clocked it from your groundskeeper's plot
as you put your supper out – paced from chair to hob,
having lost all appetite.

Would you say it was the thought of petals mushed
to muck, the senseless thud of handlebars,
the bray of callous youth

that set your fingers trembling to unlatch the case,
to take the polished body out to meet
the sullen evening air?

And all the way down
what should have been
that gift of a summer's night
was the vision of a devastated Margaret.
You thought how she'd laboured,
found and rallied volunteers –

of her bid to take the park back
to the days when she'd swim
the reservoir for a Sunday shilling,
dally at the weir bridge
to see the weekday trudge
up the valley from the pit –

of how earlier that day she'd prayed
for evening rain. Or *something*
to make park-loitering a bad idea –
her dread of the judge
and his scoring matrix
at 'Yorkshire in Bloom' the next day.

So you raged past the crazy golf,
the clown-head mouthing O,
the stunted windmill,
whose sails would whirl
some days, as your head
whirled then, would you say?

Past the mossy patron and his wife
whose stone eyes seemed to plead the way
until you reached them.
Still braying, one of them climbing
to hurl the contraption again
from the bandstand.

And you couldn't take it anymore.
You raised your gun and shot.
We don't need have the details of that.
Here we'll pull back. We'll say
you took one for the park,
for Margaret, 'Yorkshire in Bloom',
one for history, the lot.

MONOLOGUE AT AN UPSTAIRS WINDOW

after Robert Browning's 'Soliloquy of the Spanish Cloister'

He's out there trowel in hand again
among his roses, tending them
as if his kneeling at their beds
will fortify their flagging heads.
And now he strides across the grass
to check his flaccid lettuces.
If hate killed – Oh, you won't believe
he's started massaging their leaves!

At Christmas-time we get a card
inviting both of us around
for *nibbles and an Xmas drink*
and all the neighbours go and think
him philanthropically inclined
and quaff his sherry, never mind
his *local cheese* is pale and bland
and pork pies vegetarian.

And you will laugh and clink your glass
with him, along with all The Close.
How long before he drops it in
that he's just bursting for the spring?
His plans for that most sunny spot
are in full bloom – he chirps he's got
high hopes for this, the *budding year*,
with smugly non-religious cheer.

I've heard him claim to have a nook
of fairies at his garden foot
and say no one can disagree –
well, if it *is* analogy
or clever banter, tell me then
why is he cataloguing them?
I've seen him down there with a guide
and notebook flopping at his side.

And always with that same half-smile
which warms into a whistle while
he *potters* – stopping to breathe in
the glory of his gardening.
It's heartening to get outside.
He leans on gateposts satisfied
with everything – a dreary tree!
The magic of reality…

Those strawberries, if they're ready, he'll
be taking to the fete and we'll
all have to suffer him to tell
how they have grown supremely well
with just a *weeny nudge* from him.
He'll bask in praise and simpering
and you're the biggest culprit there –
you leave him beaming ear to ear.

That bulging cat from twenty-three
is lying smirking up at me –
a pellet gun would do the trick.
I wouldn't mind as much if it
would take its furry rump next-door
where it could kindly lend a paw
in burdening him with some proof,
secrete an omen in the earth.

And chicken-keeping! He has thought
of taking up that poor man's sport.
But what if they were to get free
and rampage through his celery?
Or break into his house at night
and softly stalking, feather-light,
they'll plump and climb inside his bed
and lovingly peck through his head.

He says he'd like to keep a hive
of *pollinators. O to dive
each morning in that golden jar
of breakfast-time elixir!*
If he were found with toast, face down,
the victim of an angry swarm,
they couldn't trace it back to me.
Will you laugh *then*? We'll wait and see.

MOUSE IN A GOVERNMENT BUILDING

They've had their fingers burnt before
pulling rabbits out of hats.
We stay hushed in the seams
supposing that's the reason
they are demonstrating caution.

There is a rumour that somewhere
in the future there'll be traps,
that, going forward, they are planning
to dismantle the architecture.

We hear decision dates spill by
and cabinets bulge with problems
awkward as the faces shelved inside.
Morsels are brought to the table,
seasoned talk of aims and agency.

We take stock, make fit our purpose.
In the half-light we ply and fathom
the building. We will never tell them
which treaty right we are exercising.

THE OTHER SIDE

'Just as no one can be forced into belief, so no one can be forced into
unbelief.'
– Sigmund Freud

So everything I've told you is a lie?
Get out then, or I'll call security.
I knew I couldn't trust you from the start.
It just seemed too theatrical the way
you flustered in one day and claimed
to need my second sight so badly that
I let you pay to see me privately.
Before those leaflets fell out of your bag
I had a feeling you weren't what you said.
I saw you in a hospital-like place
where everything was cold and clinical
and men in bleached bright coats stood round and laughed
and you laughed too, but not so easily.
A door stood open and you longed for air.
A forest lay beyond with birds and paths
but you resisted – there's that laugh again!

I don't know where you people get the nerve
to stamp on anything that can't be proved.
Not everything can be accounted for.
You'll learn that in your own sweet time, I'm sure.
It's Shakespeare isn't it, who says there's more
in Heaven and Earth than can be dreamt about
by us? But your lot scoff, play stupid games
and try to say my gift is trickery.
I can't be tested by you – I'm afraid
it wouldn't work. The spirits please themselves.
You can't demand they leap up and perform

and just like anyone they really hate
a smart-arse. Anyway, I've proved myself
time and again – there's a professor at
the University of Texas says
I leave him dumb and struggling for breath.

Surprise, surprise! They're friends of yours, those two
who tried to sabotage my show last month!
It makes me sick – the shameful disrespect
for the departed and their relatives.
Next thing, they're tweeting that they've scented out
a charlatan! All when I sensed their game
so fast it didn't cut it with the crowd.
The darkness and explosion wasn't theirs –
you'd realise if you'd seen that family's tears.
Now you come with another childish plan.
So then, the woman in this picture's not
your mum, or even dead – you think that proves
a point, but what? The messages I got
were meant for someone else – some poor
soul strains to reach across and to console
a grieving daughter and you barge between.

What are you? Twenty-seven, twenty-eight?
And pretty, so you don't need to resort
to trendy scientifics to turn heads.
Now wait – sit down again – I'll tell you how
this all began and how we're richer when
we keep an open mind – you've slammed yours shut
so fast it locked – who was it said don't fight
it, ride it, climb inside life's mystery?
I first made contact at the age of five.
At nursery when I innocently asked
Why was it we weren't all allowed to have

our grandads standing by us in the class,
like one girl did, the teacher went berserk
and had me spend the dinner-time shut in
an attic room with musty stacks of chairs.
But then I made some different friends in there.

And thankfully my mother came to see
that I was special, that I had the gift
she coveted. She'd sit with me, enthralled,
encourage fraternising with the dead.
She took me to a medium who knew
the score. I had a flair – and so it grew,
became a way of life, until my days
were crowded full of messages and signs.
Since then I've learnt to switch it on and off
or veil it – like this lampshade masks the bulb.
That's how I see it – one nudge and the fringe
lets fly a flash or two of radiance.
Some people, like you, fear the pure white light
and scrabble round with broken prisms – try
to make them fit – won't you at least admit
that there are different ways of knowing things?

Then take your scrappy flyers and get out
and tell your men-friends that I won't be there
this Halloween, or next – I won't defraud
the souls who need my gift with petty tests.
Sometimes they hide, sometimes I see them here
as brazen as I see you in that chair.
Go! There's the door! I have assistance on
the other side to deal with you from there.

ANTHONY TROLLOPE AND THE INVENTION OF THE PILLAR BOX

All over England,
pomaded and chignoned,
they are tripping by the dozen,
clutching billets-doux.

Hair twice what it should be,
all over the country,
vast crinolines bobbing
to boxes on corners.

Ten million fingers
release their deposits,
half-ragged with fondling
and kisses for luck.

Inside, in the darkness,
tumble epistles
to lie with their fellows
until five o'clock.

The dimness is teeming with voices:
a husband's heedful directions to his wife,
cordial business agreements, statements, receipts,
the wholesome correspondence of old ladies to their nieces.

All are besmirched in a terrible heaping
with whispers of rendezvous, free-falling compliments,
hinted elopements in high-kicking consonants,
seamless entrapments in thick creamy envelopes. Plots!

– Trollope awakes into terror and darkness,
rigid and sweat-clad beneath stiff-pressed sheets.
The blurry contours of his wife's patient slumbering
irritate and yet give some relief.

It was unfair to call those blasted boxes his invention!
Though true, their adoption the result of his enthusiasm.

Tugging at the counterpane he contemplates the young ladies of Britain,
determines on a volume for their special edification.

THE HONEYMOON

after Robert Browning's 'A Toccata of Galuppi's'

At the masked ball on the last day
in our polished wedding shoes
we danced a clutching, muddled four-step
in that alabaster hall.

Night-scent drifted through the windows
tall as ships with masts of muslin
softly veiling and unveiling
bridges racked with moon and shadow.

Waiters wound with fluted crystal
round the pristine-fronted couples.
We had barely reached our table
when the clavichordist changed his tune:

jarred the faces
jaunty or serene
set a careful skeleton
in minor key
gave it ribs to jibe and crack
the Sistine-white veneer

made it jangle
terrible and true.
I think he saw the masks
we bought that fortnight
mortal, empty-eyed and chilly
as our Decree Absolute.

TOWARDS *THE CHERRY ORCHARD*

AN ENGINE'S WHISTLE
A note from Konstantin Stanislavski to Anton Chekhov

A bright, clear, frosted morning here.
The kind that sharpens the eye,
chisels the idea.

Remember your joy at my finding
that shepherd's pipe? Its wistful
soft, insistent melody?

Well then, this: Act Two. An engine's whistle.
Lopakhin hesitates. As if in the distance,
a little train passes behind him.

I hope the difficulty in your lungs
will ease and not prevent you
coming to Moscow.

I would like to demonstrate my attempt
at that sound *heard as out of the sky,*
dying away, melancholy.

When it comes the second time
Firs is alone and we cannot tell him
from the heap of rags.

I have more thoughts on Charlotte and her dog.
And for the graveyard: the rasp of corncrakes,
a solitary frog?

Varya's keys are oversized and jangle from her belt.
Mme. Ranevskaya speaks *through her tears*
but you say she shouldn't weep?

This is not comedy, or farce. It is a tragedy,
whatever prospect of a better life you hold out
in the final act.

I feel and value every word.
There will be stillness and silences.
Let me know if we can have the little train.

THE SOUND OF A STRING BREAKING
Chekhov's response

Haymaking usually takes place
between 20 and 25 June,
at which time I think the corncrake
no longer cries.
Frogs are also silent at this time of year.

That sound – heard as out of the sky –
I shall be interested to hear
what you have planned.

Perhaps I shall write a new play
which will open like this:
How wonderful, how quiet!
Not a dog, a cuckoo,
an owl, a nightingale,
or clocks, or jingling bells.
Not even one cricket to be heard.

If you can show a train
without ANY noise,
without a SINGLE sound
then carry on.

ALLEGRA

'…and on the wall a marble tablet to be placed, with these words:
In memory of Allegra, daughter of G.G. Lord Byron, who died at
Bagnacavallo, in Italy, April 20th, 1822, Aged five years and three months.
'I shall go to her but she shall not return to me'—2d Samuel, xii, 23'
– Letter from Lord Byron regarding the burial arrangements of his daughter

I am pretty,
lively, clean.
People say
I shine
like the Milky Way.
Born in snow:
cold that day
pressed gapingly
on the window pane

but could not have its way.
Saved and sent for my Papa:
I ride with the ladies
tight in their brocades
fragrant
in their dusky skin.
We see chickens,
churches, sacks and men.

I must step
but I can run
and jump
and do at home
with other ladies;
we eat sweet nuts
powder our faces.

There came a time plain ladies stopped me.
When cold preyed in their empty rooms
and set my rose-gold hair on end
they would pretend to study
though the light had long grown grey.
Pale as turkey with its kisses

I let it have its way.
I touch fountains'
tiny coloured stones
at the bottom of their sea,
play tag in courtyard sun,
and my Papa,
I go to him
for he did not return to me.

THE YELLOW HOUSE

FISHERMEN'S CRADLE

Vincent Van Gogh to Paul Gauguin, Arles, December 1888.
The picture is Van Gogh's 'The Lullaby'.

Madame Roulin in this picture holds the string
that rocks the cradle, lulls its occupants,
in mind of songs their mothers used to sing.

She pulls the thread and watches day advance
until a single star pins up the sky;
a dawn as Rousseau or Daubigny paints.

You think Rousseau's mornings nothing, but the way
the Barbizons catch nature – I could weep!
How can you shrug at such sad majesty?

Are we to take a walk before we sleep?
Perhaps a brandy at old Ginoux's place.
Our funds can stretch to that – and it might keep

the Horla from my room – buy us some peace.
You know I'm better stunned against the storm,
the only time these roaring colours cease.

Inside the crib the fishermen are warm
and rocked yet tethered by this mother's pull.
Forgetful of the catch they stretch and yawn.

Thick tendrils creep along the nursery wall,
between them dahlias rear up and stare,
but Mother Roulin keeps watch over all.

Where are you going? Can I meet you there?
The evening air will be a salve to me.
At least say you won't go beyond the square!

I'll follow him and beg for clemency.

THE EXECUTION OF PRADO

Paul Gauguin, January 1889, on his return to Paris after staying with Van Gogh in the Yellow House in Arles.

And still I have not had the sleep I'm due
for as we smoked and talked in Place Pigalle
that notice from the city guard came through
informing us of the impending death
by guillotine of Prado. Murderer
he may indeed have been, he held himself
in just the manner of a character
from Zola or a Balzac tragedy.
We doubted they could snuff him out so easily.

So I and Shuffernecker made our way
across the town to stamp our numbing feet
beneath the grimy square of starless sky.
But Christ how long they kept us captive there
before they even brought out the machine!
Another hour before the man himself
was dragged on to complete the tawdry scene.
They need not have demeaned him with their chains;
he bore the spectacle with weary insolence –

until the blade came down upon his nose.
He roared and cursed his executioners,
who blanched and bustled with the shaft and ropes
and forced his shoulders back onto the block
until his shaven head lay in the box.
It could have been the jute they lined it with;
the blood thick as impasto on the gauze,
perhaps the violent sloping of his brow,
but I was put in mind of Vincent and of Arles.

And having not yet slept since coming here
and travelled arduously all yesterday,
my brain feels full of that strange atmosphere,
as bristling as the air before a storm.
I think I'm seeing Vincent everywhere,
still smell the oily pungence of that house,
as glaring yellow as the wheat fields there
and just as dark and creaking at its heart;
a livid place where dreams and nightmares come apart.

Well, you have had a whiff of what went on,
how no one would come near, towards the end.
The evenings were unconscionably long.
The children even stopped tormenting him
as if they somehow sensed him on the brink.
Don't push me any further on it now.
I feel so weary I can hardly think.
I'll drain this final tumbler and retire
with neither stamina nor stomach, nor desire.

MISS LAMB IS FROM HOME

The gardens every morning when
the sky is slurred a dawnish mauve
are pressed to winter's temples then
a dense and dreary stillness wove.
The buried snowdrop cannot rouse
the will to break its bulbous doze
and no one comes and no one goes
about the darkly guarded house.

When spring is here I swear I'll love her.
When she's here I know I'll be
home from home and with my brother.
I'll take him rue and rosemary.

The black-barked boughs accuse the sky
of cudgelling their furniture.
Amongst the shrivelled shrub-work I
proceed, a frightful Perdita.
The February flowerbed lies
quite naked by the chicken coop,
the red-legged birds in wait to stoop
to pluck the violets' sweet, dim eyes.

When spring is here I swear I'll love her.
When she's here I'll go and see
a play or two with my dear brother.
What a merry pair we'll be.

O Proserpina, for the flowers
that, frighted, you let tumble free,
I'd give the moon, meek at this hour

and Quaker white as chastity.
Indeed, at this discreet address
a dozen lofty Angelos
are constant in pursuit of those
unlucky to be brotherless.

When Spring is here these grounds will freeze on.
When she's here I do not know
if I will be. O Brother, come,
replant me while my sap is low.

2.
SOMEWHERE
TO GET TO

BUILDING

Crossing the ocean sealed in a tin can is no fun:
the darkness and nausea – dread of it coming to an end.
Everything piecework of the shuddering torchlight,
blind trust in the bastards to remember something
is breathing down in the hold. Thank Christ today
I work the skyline, buoyed up by the noisy air.

When the lorry doors were levered open
we arched and scrambled like cats from a sack.
But from up here, looking back, better that
we were uncovered. Questioned for hours
about home and why we left and why we came.
For the first time someone writing it down.

I said to myself come Hell I was not going back.
I would find a thing to do. Never frightened by heights,
as a child from the top of the tallest tree
I gazed down on the mischief of others:
the sleights of women, lies of men,
the pedlar's bells and curses rising up to me.

The date of my hearing slipped – kept sliding
until one day someone with a suit and committee
signed a treaty that changed things for me.
Rules were translated to the language of my country.
Since then I must have rendered half this city
and the drills ring in my bones now
with the pedlar's hard-flung charm.

TOAST

I open a window,
watch someone walking dully along.

The day is wide and bright-cracked grey.
The mail arrives:
sharp-edged cellophane cascade.

Today
I will go into the city.
It will be enormous,
someone always in my way.

I cram the heel of bread
into the toaster's stiff
and tarnished grate.

The feathered wax of butter melts.

I catch myself,
drop the plate.

THE BENJAMIN NEWTON

After Degas' *The Absinthe Drinkers*

The drain's reek pushes us out of our building again.
He says they are mulched to the rim
with gulped-down dreams of the hopeless.
I think something shuffled in, bedded-down
and died in them.

And now we are here:
backs to the wall with the mirror,
ordering coffee, sitting like penitents
over the dregs of it more than an hour. No one's
complaining, no one demanding we face up
to the international situation.

I am considering absinthe
the green of city bridges' sub-terrain,
how the gauze of the window sets a haze on the drizzle,
the grimy mechanical churning of coins
from the arcade next-door's gloom. We order drinks,
will try to ride the downturn.

He says who can know
we will not do something brave and spontaneous tomorrow?
That we won't all suddenly throw down the reins
and shaking our heads clear leap from the merry-go-round?
But then the slurred and whirring tunes
well up again next door

and I know I'm the woman in the mirror behind
and the monkey and cymbals and the organ's grind.

VIEW BACK

This drizzling morning's wait has set me off along the narrow gauge
      to Dungeness.
The power station's looming hull should be enough to put the brakes on
but we press across the swept expanse; the shingle bank our guidebook calls
the second largest in the world. Half-visible a pub sign stakes its claim:
The only pub in Dungeness.

But we can't stop. It's 1983. The dockyard's on the brink of closure
and there's no station after Romney Sands. The dockyard's dead and done
but do we know that yet, in 1983? It's spring I think. It's hard to see
the detail through the mist. We settle for the names of promised things:
grey willow catkin, butterburr.

Come afternoon Dad forks out hard for tokens outside Dymchurch fair.
I forge their imprint in my palm and stand before the Crooked House.
Inside the dark arcade the two pence pushers heave their shelves
of coppers back and forth. We stare, imagining the clatter and the
      shocking glory
of the tipping point.

If only all the prizes weren't impossible to win. I dream a tumbling
      cliff of teddies.
Still, we'll comb the strandline if the weather clears, chuck seaweed
and play chicken, writing swear words in the sand behind Dad's back.
He stands and looks as if he sees right through the murk across the headland
to the lighthouse and beyond.

But it's the train ride that this drizzling morning's sent me on. My father
hunched inside. We can see nothing till it's right on top of us.
The homeward leg will drag us past the yards of houses. Washing strung along,
back doors as private as the deals we didn't want, but lived with,
to this drizzling day.

MINUTE TAKER

Tuesday, 10.20.
Pitstop at staff kitchen.
The window chock-fuck-full
of damn ducks.

This building's fancy curvature
is unsuited to the pruned
and plumbed-in venture of
the modern business.

The architect's a maudlin bastard.
Impenitent and far away
and done with plans.
Long shuffled off.

The pimped ex-stockroom's
malty backmost portion
juts eye-level onto this:
a reed-webbed weir

where city ducks clamber –
fuck! –
re-clamber
to the top.

Once up
they ponce and showboat,
flick their arses
at the plunge back down.

I roll the minutes of the previous meeting,
hold them to the hollow of my eye.
Avast ye ducks! I'm gathering momentum.

A whoosh, a splash,
a scramble and rebalancing.
Apologies. We are all transitioning.

There will be amendments,
gratuitous and indignant.
But I'm rallying now with the volley of quacks.

CIVIC SPACE

after Katherine Mansfield

The Casual Play Worker gathers them round:
These are the plants that the dinosaurs ate.
We are going to paint them – wait!

But they're bursting full of squawks
and drop haphazardly in groups
across the sunny glasshouse paths.

Above, in the arid, open space
great blades cut time, cool and precise.
Cameras on arched beams swivel and shine.

Next door they're building a hotel.
A yellow crane robustly hoists,
egg-yolk hardhats scoot below.

Back down here on the hothouse floor
Soup of the Day is Organic Carrot.
Lunch-breakers absentmindedly navigate.

A City Centre Ambassador
stands blinking by the refreshment bar.
Her City Council insignia

flaring now and then in the filtered sun.
She waits, packed up with civic knowledge.
The place will shut at five o'clock.

Meanwhile the pre-school pterodactyls
squabble and swoop over yellows and greens.
One of them squeals through the cycad leaves

seeing the glaring gold eye of a *big* dinosaur!
Another stares upwards silently watching
the crane swing its load like the meteor.

FEAST

'Big savouries for modest pockets!"

Another wet lunch like this
could finish me off.
The rows of baguettes cling
wretchedly to their iceberg,
pizzas weep their virgin oil

while you stew in your offices,
scrabbling for change
for the snack machine,
nipping to the canteen,
unwrapping something
you've brought from home.

You used to come down.
You know I make you welcome.

Why do you think this tank of pasties
sadly turn their bed of grease-proof paper clear?
Because there is no one here
to clutch them warm and eagerly away.

I stare at the pin board of missing persons,
trying to decipher their preferences.
Perhaps today will be the day they'll all
make a return. Come home, my friends.
A pie makes a reunion complete.

BLUEPRINT

Each day I wave the crusted lorries through
from a cabin at the mouth of it
and watch them shunt and tilt and spew
their cargo in the designated pit.

And picture more already deepening
in city bins – with last night's carcass gone,
let's start again with freshly emptied coffee cups,
new dog ends, tickets wedged with chewing gum.

So someone in a kitchen cannot face
the heel of toast or finds a primal urge
to scour the fridge clean, till the weekly purge
is done with, wheeled through gennels to the curb.

I keep this soiled outskirt of the town,
the company of gulls through every day.
They circle in and claw each reeking mound,
unruffled by the five-year strategy:

the plan that sets out what is to become
of this place when we've stuffed its gaping guts,
and the regulation treatment's calmed it down,
they've monitored the gases, sewn it up.

The blueprints show apartment blocks that stare
at *tranquil, stunning,* strangely fenced-off heath,
their surcharge-paying tenants unaware
of the fetid city gizzards underneath.

IN WHICH THE PIECES ARE PUT TOGETHER

The art of the jigsaw puzzle at first glance
seems insubstantial; easily swept aside
by a simple introduction to Gestalt.

Mr Happy is enjoying a picnic in the park,
roundly reclining on a checked blanket
next to the bright blue lake.

We need to find the edges first.
She hurls a fistful of the little chaps
at the guarded fortress of the fireplace.

The pieces disappear, cease to exist
as pieces. Perec says we should see
the puzzle-maker as the other player.

Although water skiing seems inadvisable
for one so chronically prone to misadventure,
Mr Bump is giving it a go.

This is a blind-cut cardboard affair
bought from The Works at the threat of a tantrum.
The sun through the window is also mollifying.

The only thing that counts, says Perec,
is the ability to link one piece
to another. We are moving closer.

The uncomfortably vibrant brown
turns out to be Mr. Uppity, holding court.
That murky rim, thankfully, his monocle.

The living room carpet doesn't bear scrutiny.
I am working towards one. Great. Thought.
A vacuum might be the fix we need.

Stripped of their signifying power again,
the Mr Men become chewable adumbrations.
She bites her own toe and roars for justice.

STANDARD DOUBLE

The suite sucked clean
prepared again
a welcome greeting
programmed on its plasma screen

the laundry trolley
harried with its dirty linen
firmly rolled
anonymous off left.

The next checked-in
hadn't planned to sleep alone
flicks off the name
unfaithful on the screen

stares out at the cloud
bunking up in the suburbs
looks in and is spited
by the touches in the bathroom:

the spotlight, that soap-stack
stuck up with a ribbon
left perched by the mirror
like a fucking valentine.

CONKEROR

a specular

My father had a mania for
those implements of petty war.
In my satchel they would lie, braced,
extracted from a shock-blue sky.
In the blazoned hall,
tormented by Monday Assembly,
I would recall

how he intercepted that slicing drop:
hands rigged above his head,
nostrils flared capillary red,
sun-squinting though the leaves.
A missile hurled into the tree –

a thorned case caught and handed solemnly to me.

A missile hurled into the tree.
Sun squinting through the leaves,
nostrils flared capillary red,
hands rigged above his head,
how he intercepted that slicing drop.

I cannot help recall,
tormented by mundane assembly
in this corporate hall,
distracted by a shock-blue sky.
In memory they lie, braced;
those implements of petty war
my father had a mania for.

ALLGEMEINBILDUNG

(German, meaning: everything that an adult capable of living independently
can reasonably be expected to know)

That frozen sausages thrown
into a hot pan will spit
scaldingly.

That painting kitchen cupboards
brightly and with stencils
will not result in a playful
boho chic.

That it's wise to feign business as usual
for the over-eager neighbour
and not to let her in too much.

That it is difficult to ascertain
(even for the professional)
when a person has been re-abled.

That from here on the floor
the man whose kitchen
looks into mine
can't see me.

That beauty is, by and large
a simple matter of symmetry.

That wonky stencils and a shaking hand
probably won't produce symmetry.

That pain can do strange things
to the mind and body.

That it's warm and dark
in the uterus and perhaps the baby
never really wants to come out anyway.

That cats don't care if you live or die
and won't go for help in an emergency.

That unmopped lino
mulched with month-old crumbs
is surprisingly, numbingly, comfy.

That if something is missing for long enough
it is almost certainly behind the fridge.

That, in the absence of answers,
nodding, saying nothing, hiding
is the holy trinity.

That the scars from scalding sausages
do not disappear overnight.

That if something is missing for long enough
it is almost certainly not behind the fridge.

COMMUTER

He had considered moving to the city,
but realised one day, or rather, evening,
that all he really knew there was the station

and the girl – should he say woman?
– with her latte and her muffin
and just the time to sit and eat them
in the lurid light of Café Pumpkin;

who draped her coat over the orange acrylic,
went with the hang-dog patter of the assistant,
and in an instant, coat re-buttoned, could become
Celia Johnson, prim amid the crowd
on the canopied platform.

He knew how the train would come,
how everyone would edge jealously forward,
hating Cityliving counterparts
already home behind high windows
square as post-it notes

or how, to their dismay, a voice would
proclaim, quite unremorsefully,
it was sorry to announce the delay…

WE DO NOT MENTION

We do not mention that the meat was tough
and rise before the streaky plates congeal
to do the washing-up and then make love.

I show compassion that your day was rough
and long. Not wanting to reach overkill
we do not mention that the meat was tough.

Dessert was not what I'd been dreaming of:
Iced-cream in see-through plastic tubs. Oh well,
we'll do the washing-up and then make love.

At dinner, when I said I'd had enough,
you looked like hell and asked if I was ill.
I did not mention that the meat was tough.

Though, grimacing, you grip the scouring cloth,
and marigolds don't add to your appeal,
we'll do the washing-up and then make love.

You wash, I dry and put away the stuff,
and in this squeaky, slippery silence still
we do not mention that the meat was tough,
just do the washing-up and then make love.

YOU ARE CHARLOTTE AT ROE HEAD

Lying here, hands folded in the coffin style,
unshut curtains letting in the petrol station's glow,
breathe deep and refute, as she would,
the relentless prattle: the ornamental lisping
of the girls below.

The dormitory is high and airy-wide but try conceiving
a longing for the confinement of the parsonage.
The spectre of Branwell uncanny in the hall.
The narrow windows channelling the vastness
of the moor.

At Roe Head, shrouded in the greyness of your dress,
you brook the hours at your class-front desk,
each day take the part of the stern church-mouse,
burying deep the exuberant ease and candour
of your home character.

These evenings, mired, feel how you are
a passenger in a waking nightmare.
No better company than a stalking ghost,
you might apologise years later in a letter
to Miss Woolner.

Yet evenings are the only time you own:
thoughts climb up, as from the dark walls of a well.
Knocked back by day they fall and petrify.
Swallowing your grief, you lift your eyes up
to the hills —

But now keep still – the girls are on their way
to fetch their combs and curling papers,
elbowing and prating purple versions of the day.
So you, and she, in the growing gloom, remain unseen
as they come clamouring in.

3.
CLAIMS – VOICES
FROM THE GREAT
INUNDATION OF 1864

Round about midnight on March 11th 1864
the Dale Dyke Dam at Bradfield, near Sheffield, collapsed,
releasing a torrent of water that killed some 250 people. It
devastated an area that stretched from the dam, down the
Loxley Valley, through Malin Bridge and Hillsborough, to
Sheffield town centre and beyond. Following the disaster,
compensation claims were made by individuals and
companies against the Sheffield Water Company
for loss of property and livelihood, and for
injury or death of relatives.

WARNING AT THE BARREL INN

Mr. Fountain sent his son, Stephenson Fountain, on horseback to Sheffield, to tell Mr. Gunson to come to the reservoir as soon as possible, as there was a crack in the embankment; and off the young man rode as fast as the darkness of the night, the fury of the tempest, and the mountainous nature of the road would permit.

What a terrible slip –
I hoped not to lose time,
entrusted on such a grand errand as this.

Being driven two miles
by the thundering gales,
I was set to impress with the time that I made

but treacherous scree
and a dark, downward course
broke my damned horse's saddle girth!

I'll not take a flagon, Sirs, thank you the same.
Momentarily only my ride is postponed.
I fly on the moment my beast is returned!

Nay, this rain does not slow down one jot.
You fellows may do well to keep
your bacchanalian antics up!

What a different scene at the reservoir.
My father does his utmost to assure
that it is but an innocent crack
…that is…fissure –

even now the men still bend and puzzle,
squint their hardest with hoisted lamp,
my father explaining over them that
it is simply the inner part of the embankment,
twixt the water and the puddle wall,
how does he put it? *Subsiding* a little,
that there really is no call for fright,
no present danger – though some gents
do not heed his words at all!

So I am sent to satisfy their frets,
to fetch and deliver the chief engineer,
all the way from his West Street townhouse
where I warrant he'll not welcome being roused!
Yet I would be a fool indeed to shrink
from such a chance to prove my mettle and
– my horse!

Oh Gentlemen, please,
do not stir from your seats.
Proceed in your former, most jovial, stream!

I have spoken
not to alarm but inform –

with God's speed
I may not stop again
'til these hooves greet the ear of Mr Gunson!

THE BALLAD OF MRS KIRK

In the house of Thomas Kirk and his wife lodged one who neglected the warning of the flood: Henry Burkinshaw, known as Sheffield Harry.

I knew the evening he arrived
we'd taken in a fool,
as taking from the drawer a spoon
I'd chanced to let it fall.

It hit the floor, gave out a clang,
its bowl stared up at me –
a shining silver omen which
foretold catastrophe.

Oh Sister, from your coastal home,
enjoy this narrative.
I'll tell you the particulars
now you're assured we live!

★★★

I felt, the evening of the flood,
a dread chill through and through:
my Thomas and our neighbour paced
as if the talk were true.

Our lodger, Harry Burkinshaw
burst in with all his fuss.
He laughed at their queer, ghostly looks
and scoffed, proclaiming thus:

'A dozen grown men squint and squawk,
around a cavity
so minor that I'll eat my hat
and coat before I flee!'

They pressed him but he brushed them off.
'There's nothing to be done –
the reservoir is more than safe;
I know the ombudsman!'

So, with a flourish, off to bed
old Harry swept instead.
My Thomas and our neighbour sat;
I took them tea and bread.

The fire made their eyes burn bright
and hints of present danger
made me shudder in my sweeping and
retire to my chamber.

★★★

Not upward of an hour had
I washed and said my prayers:
a most ungodly thumping seemed
to come from next door's stairs.

Then Thomas dashed into the room
and swiftly out again
half-screaming 'Love, we must depart –
we'll drown if we remain!'

Between us then we roused the house
and made an urgent plea

to leave no matter what their state,
to forego modesty!

In states of varying undress
across the bridge we fled.
Why, Mrs Walton from next door
 was carried in her bed!

Just then as I was scrambling safe
it came into my head,
to my great horror, I had left
poor Tim and Tabs for dead!

★★★

So back across the iron bridge,
still nightgown-clad, I race,
and no one sees to stop me on
that thronging hill's dark face.

Dear quivering Tim I gladly grab
from out his little shack,
and finding still a candle lit,
upstairs to save my cat!

I drag her out from underneath
my bed, rebuke her hiss –
then comes a gruff, uncivil voice:
'What damned commotion's this?'

'Oh, Mr. Burkinshaw!' I cry
'Is that you still in bed?'
No time to harken at his door,
I throw it wide instead.

He's by his elbows half propped up
and gaping in surprise,
adorned in striped nightgown and cap –
Wee-Willy-Winky-wise!

'Oh Mr. Burkinshaw' I chide –
'You must get out of bed.
The dam has burst, the water comes –
the other lodgers fled!'

His only answer is a snort.
I turn with puss and hound.
Have I not, Sister, often said
I thought his mind unsound?

Yet, as I glance back from the hall,
'though muttering and mocking,
I do believe he's made a move
and seized one worsted stocking.

But Tim and Tabs and I cannot
delay one moment more.
I clasp them, one beneath each arm,
and stagger to the door.

And as we pass the parlour – oh –
I scarce can find the words
to tell you I had no hand free
to fetch my poor song birds!

Across the bridge once more I dash.
The river roars beneath
so violently to gain the bank
brings very great relief.

No sooner have we laid our feet
and paws upon the ground,
than roll a thousand thunder claps
that echo all around!

And louder still and louder still
and nearer draws the thunder.
We scramble farther up the bank
and turn and gawp in wonder –

Between the hills there slides a huge
and horrifying sight:
a roaring, foaming, monstrous thing.
It charges with such might
that trees are snapped and barns upturned
and carried through the night!

And for a time the valley holds
a violent, thrashing tide
just like a giant's peggy-tub,
and everything inside,
with tree trunks turned to dolly poles,
is rattled and destroyed.

The bridge is lost – our house stands up
for just a moment more –
then shudders and is dashed away
as if built out of straw.

The awful wash-load tumbles on
and pounds the countryside
and nothing in its path can duck
a terrifying ride

The noise subsides and up go cries
lamenting foolish Harry.
He had his chance and wouldn't budge –
I mourn my poor canary.

★★★

Well, Sister – Tim and Tabs and I,
and Thomas, now reside
in Neepsend, by the tanneries,
which I cannot abide!

So, how I long to visit you
and take the Blackpool air,
to stroll the front and watch the gulls,
brush sea-spray from our hair!

And 'though you rave about that great
attraction built this year –
I don't think, after my near miss,
it wise to risk the pier!

A HEAD CLERK'S HOUSE

'…the ruins were such as to strike the mind of the visitor with wonder that the destruction should have gone so far and yet have stopped where it did.'

So any passer-by may see the way
his house stands gaping – frontage at its feet!
Who would have thought he'd come to work today

sails full of wind as ever! When he lay
our orders down we kept our winks discreet
'though any passer-by may see the way

things were within his kingdom yesterday;
the quilling on his bed, each royal pleat.
To condescend to come to work today!

Such stock of silverware, they start to say,
was managed through some elegant deceit
and simple passers-by may see the way

each collar, cuff and front, pressed to obey,
hangs rigid and meticulously neat
and still hang those ordained for work today!

His home's a doll's house – any eye may play
across the scene, pulled open for the street
and every passer-by must guess the way
his savvy-faire will not quite work today!

THE SERMON AND THE TRAIL OF SIN

'Local and District News – The Surrey Theatre – Other and more important
engagements have prevented our usual notices of this place of amusement for
the past week. The principal novelty is a new drama of the modern sensation
school entitled 'The Trail of Sin'.'

St Stephen's was popular yesterday night.
The Reverend's sermon most dreadfully good!
How we all listened appalled and transfixed
as he told of the terrible work of the flood.

He took up the Bible with fire in his eyes
and bade us think closely of Luke, Chapter 8.
For all who were mawkish or burdened by loss,
he would inquire of them 'Where is your faith?'

Just like the disciples when crossing the lake
we had to forbear and put trust in the Lord.
The late Visitation was not wholly bad:
the proud had been humbled and meekness restored.

Were you at the Trickett girls' May Dance last year?
Can you quite believe they lie cold in the ground?
I felt rather odd when the Reverend told how
the swine, full of devils, were driven and drowned.

The candles were fancy and never so tall –
the forms which they threw on the windows, exquisite!
I never saw so many flowers before.
Our faces looked buoyant – becomingly lit!

I chided myself with rebukes most severe
and prayed for the wretched with all of my might,

but all of that talk of the Fallen and Sin
had put me in mind of the theme for tonight!

And Reverend Burbidge up there at the front
had somehow the look of tonight's leading man –
but not such fine whiskers – and even more stern,
with his warning that frivolous revellers are damned!

He would not approve of tonight's play, I fear –
would frown on your feathers – although they are sweet –
and go so excessively well with that gown!
The theatre's so crowded now! Where is your seat?

GEORGE

'All the inmates of the Workhouse were in bed except a young man in charge of the boiler house. He is an imbecile, and known only by the name of George.'

I confess, Mr Wescoe, I stopped my work
when I heard the roar of the Devil through the dark
and I climbed up onto the boiler house top
and whistled to keep my courage up.

I confess Mr Wescoe, I saw Matron Day
throw up her window across the way
and when she asked me what I heard
I answered truly, to please the Lord.

I said 'I do not know, I do not know,'
and only smiled for Matron's sake.
Ladies like to be comforted in that way,
as you always say, Mr Wescoe.
But I do not know, I do not know
why the waters began to rise.
The tanks were always attended to.
They're saying it was a sign.
Do you think so, Mr Wescoe?

But, see Sir, it wasn't me it came for –
for the waters started on the lowest floor
where those ladies you so often tell me about,
the ones with improper morals, are housed.

I couldn't move from the boiler house top
and whistled to keep my courage up
and I didn't aid the ladies' rescue
but my soul is as white as yours, Mr Wescoe.

THE APOTHECARY'S WIDOW: A SENSATION STORY

Come now, you did not ride half way 'cross town
to stand on ceremony, pray, sit down.
Let Sarah take from you your hat and coat
and bring us tea. I read with haste the note
you sent and scarce could take it in at first –
then how my bosom trembled! I rehearsed
what I should say when you arrived to seek
an explanation. Sir, I want to speak
as artlessly as possible, and have
you grasp the circumstance that made me crave
such dark solutions. So, it seems you've turned
detective and, as thus, suppose you've earned
the privilege to peer inside my heart,
to scrutinise my conscience, prize apart
each scruple for inspection, place it back
beside my soul – which you think Brunswick-black!
I fought to quell my raging passion's claims
as the vessel curbs its substance, over flames.
Shall I now hold myself aloft for you,
that you may judge this fragile phial's hue?

My husband, your dear brother, was a man
devoted to his work. He often ran
his business into hours of the night;
preparing orders, setting papers right.
That fateful night he came to me and stood
before my cheval-glass. He said he could
not from his work retire, despite the time.
This made him sorry, but if I would climb
into our bed then just to leave me safe

and sound would bring a measure of relief.
So this I did, insisting that he take
the wine I had decanted. It would make
his arduous labours lighter as he sipped.
He praised my soft attentiveness and slipped
then from the house. I upped and dressed,
for once not musing this or that gown best,
drew fast my hooded cloak against the cold,
foreboding dark, and desperate now to hold
my nerve and hoping that revenge was sweet
as bergamot, I plunged into the street.

The town felt larger than it does by day.
I shrank into my cloak and kept at bay
the dread by concentrating on my feet.
How small they looked and sounded as they beat
the cobbled lanes. At length I came upon
the shop. A thick, warm glow like honey shone
forth, cloying in the gutter, and within
I saw two figures: *she* was there with him!
'Though I had known what I would find, the sight
still turned my gut. To see they thought me quite
as green as a tureen of turtle soup
and safe tucked up at home in bed – to stoop
to such foul depths! The blood roared in my veins!
I clutched the window ledge, peeped through the panes,
and crouching now, could see the real work he
pursued inside that nasty nectary!
Amid the shelves of tinctures, bulbous glass
with tall and tear-dropped stoppers, gaudy casks
inscribed with names of wicked-sounding goods:
Venetian Red, Boiled Oil and Dragon's Blood,
I spied the wine which I had pressed on him –
unstoppered yet, still potent to the brim!

My gaze fell on their honeying once more –
I must have fainted clean away and for
some minutes lay a sad and crumpled heap.
When I awoke I found I could not keep
the sound of raging tempests from my brain,
yet through the dismal streets I flew again
not stopping until Sarah took my cloak.
I need not paint the scene the town awoke
to the next morn – you *know* how they were found,
my husband and a nameless *other*, drowned!

Sir, you are death-mask white and do not wield
your former knowledge now that I've revealed
my desperate scheme that God would not let be.
Ah, Sarah brings the tray – you'll take some tea?

A FURTHER LAMENTATION OF THE LATE INUNDATION AND ENSUING CLAIMS FOR COMPENSATION

After Richard Nesbit Ryan: Late Theatrical Manager; Now Author, Poet and Publisher

'Twas a dark and stormy night in wildest March.
The nightingale shuddered in the larch.
All Sheffield snored from Moorfoot to the Wicker Arch.

No man can be in doubt and ask 'Of which night do you speak?'
Nor woman neither – 'though some believe the fairer sex in intellect are weak!
'Twas the night a roaring, watery beast seized the Loxley valley in its beak!

Oh, innocent Sheffield and each sweet north-westerly district,
The appalling damage done to you, my former ode on this theme does depict.
And the great unrest of these post-diluvian months did I predict.

Such loss of life and property has rarely e'er been seen.
A great deal of time and money will be, or has already been,
Spent recovering goods and bodies and getting our toll roads clean.

Now our munificent Mayor and considerate Corporation,
In the light of the scale of the terrible devastation
Have persevered in negotiating us town-folk compensation.

For although we are sure the Water Company took utmost care,
It was they who did build the reservoir there,
So along with Mother Nature, they the blame must share.

So a three-man commission at the Town Hall will sit
Lead by William Overend QC, they will award as they see fit
And decipher each and every case with eruditious wit.

First they might take a butcher's claim.
Why, how can he carry his business on the same
With his livestock drowned and his eldest son lame?

Then a widow's case is brought to the fore.
Her clothes and furniture were lost, and what is more,
Her house made aqueous from chimney to floor!

For these good and piteous creatures, the Commissioners, we see
Employ a gracious amount of compassion and sympathy –
Both are sent away – with fair and ample fee!

But who's this now taking centre stage?
A hawker – whose list of damages exceeds a page!
Claiming all manner of commodities from silk cravat to gilded cage!

The Commissioners confabulate a while and finally say
'This kind of churlish villain over us will not hold sway!'
The case, with due repugnance, is directly sent away.

That foolish hawker his chance for recompense hath missed,
Through the crafty compilation of such a gross, inflated list.
I say that he is justly served – his case being dismissed!

As the days march bravely on, our three wise men shall see
Many-a-and-important case relating to local industry:
Sheffield's famous manufacturers bereft of time and property.

Messrs. Ibbotson and Company, of the world-renowned Globe Works,
Your great factory was halted, round each dark corner more expense lurk
Yet you do pay the weekly wages of your idle smiths and absent clerks.

Of Neepsend's noble tanneries – Mr. Fawley's was hard hit.
His hides and hackles sullied; for further treatment, are unfit.
They languish, slayed a second time, in an inundated pit.

But Little Mesters and Grand Masters up and down our Sylvan glen
Do not fret upon the judgement – You are dealing with such men
As our three grand commissioners, who most fairly wield their pen!

I, myself, sustained a bitter, cruel and most pernicious blow!
But being men of culture and of elevated taste I know
That panel will rule justly and recognition of my labours show.

There is, for instance, my ode celebrating
John Brown and Co's great armour plating
All copies of which were swept through my roof (despite superior slating).

Messrs. Stanleys' monster anvil block still stands, thank goodness,
       broad and true.
Yet my ode on its great majesty – Alas, what has become of you?
My long, painstaking memoir has been rent asunder too!

My famous poems on places – I hear the populace cry 'What of them?'
They are lost! Ay, e'en the favourites; those on Bakewell, Wentworth,
       Rotherham.
For the Board I bind a thorough list, 'though it pains me much to
       bother them.

And so to all who mean to put in claims – by all means be meticulous.
But should you feel inclined to cheat, remember how conspicuous
You will appear – and end up most reviled and ridiculous.

It may be just a panshon – or some trousers – but forefend!
Shame the devil, make him howl! Refuse the truth to bend!
Thus raise yourself in the esteem of William Overend (QC).

THE PARTICULARS

'All claimants are to provide sufficient detail as to the particulars and nature of their loss. All claims are to be heard and settled by the Commissioners, who have the authority to approve, negotiate or dismiss all claims.'

Earthenware of various sorts:
bottles, pancheons, a maiden pot.
A besom and an oil cloth.
All of which I'm afraid were washed
from my dwelling house and lost.

A pair of boots and workbox.
Stuff dresses and plain petticoats,
one woollen shawl, two trunks
of fancy drapery, a silk umbrella –
the latter items came to me by my late mother.

Three small ornaments in the parlour,
an old but very comfortable chair
with nicely embroidered antimacassar
which cannot have been worth so much
as that I do not know that I can get another.

Quite a quantity of Britannia goods
belonging to the owner of Love Street Works
who employs me as an outworker,
to engrave and buff his teapots,
which I did my best to salvage and recover.

Other unfortunate articles in my care:
in the yard John Jepson's deals of timber,
Mr Bagnall's donkey's supply of straw.
Unluckily, a case of gin and one of porter –
which I was looking after for my brother.

I feel certain there are other items
which I cannot at this present time
quite bring to the forefront of my mind
or have forgotten.

.

CLAIM FOR MARY ANN PICKERING, AGED 8

Made by Alfred Pickering, Saw Grinder, Creswick Street, Langsett Road.

The memory of my 'foresaid daughter
is, by the late flood, much impaired.
She starts and raves about the water.
Her spirit's low and all seems marred.

She was residing with my brother,
above the public house he kept.
What now remains of his endeavour?
The attic corner where she slept.

I do indeed attempt to rouse her
from out her melancholic state.
We walk out when the mood allows her.
I take home figs and ha'penny cake.

I read this morning from the paper
of Whitsuntide festivities
and promised if I could I'd take her,
reeled off the curiosities –

gymnasts and vaulters
clowns and nimble jugglers
pipers and conjurers
acrobats to turn the mind
bears who lumber and delight
a helter-skelter decked and bright
jollity of every kind –
and everything together
in the warm whit weather –

paddling for tiny-foots
Daring-David swing-boats
titbits for sweet-tooths;
lozenges of green and yellow
candied rinds for the eager hands
of open-faced little fellows!

But still a dark cloud passes over.
The pantomime may seem grotesque,
the shadow puppets loom like phantoms.
What of the contortionist?

At best, I fear it will not cure her
and by the evening she'll forget
and only rave about the water
and cry that it may get her yet.

NOTES AND ACKNOWLEDGEMENTS

Thanks are due to the editors of the following publications in which some of these poems first appeared: *Antiphon, The Boston Review, English, The Interpreter's House, Matter, Other Poetry, Prole, The Rialto, The SHOp, Ten Hallam Poets,* and *The Wolf.*

Thanks must go to Sean and Teddy for their support, encouragement, forbearance, and for all manner of trifles.

Massive thanks also to my parents and to Linda Lee Welch, Elizabeth Barrett, Suzannah Evans, Beverley Nadin, Mark Doyle, Angelina D'Roza, Katharine Towers, Chris Jones, Steve Earnshaw, Kate Parry, and others, for all your advice, support and enthusiasm. Finally, a thank you must go to the Eyewear team.

MEN, WOMEN AND MICE:
TOWARDS *THE CHERRY ORCHARD*

'The sound of a string breaking' is something of a found poem. I have pieced together lines from Chekhov's correspondence and added a few lines of my own. I used Chekhov's words to imagine the letter which prompted them: 'An engine's whistle' is a fictitious letter from *The Cherry Orchard*'s director, Konstantin Stanislavski.

MISS LAMB IS FROM HOME

In 1796 Mary Lamb stabbed her mother to death. She was not imprisoned or otherwise punished, but placed in the care of her brother, Charles. For the next forty years the siblings lived and worked together, most famously co-writing *Tales from Shakespeare*. They lived, however, in the shadow of Mary's recurring bouts of mental illness, which meant she was usually confined to an asylum for several months each year. Her brother euphemistically referred to this as her being 'from home'.

CLAIMS - VOICES FROM THE GREAT INUNDATION OF 1864
The explanatory paragraph is reproduced with the kind permission of the Sheffield Flood Claims Archive at Sheffield Hallam University (https://www2.shu.ac.uk/sfca/).

Most of the poems are prefaced with either a snippet from *A Complete History of the Great Flood at Sheffield* by Samuel Harrison (1864) or claimant details from the Sheffield Flood Claims Archive.

OO EYEWEAR PUBLISHING